Migrating to Cloud-Native Application Architectures

Matt Stine

Beijing · Cambridge · Farnham · Köln · Sebastopol · Tokyo

Migrating to Cloud-Native Application Architectures

by Matt Stine

Copyright © 2015 O'Reilly Media. All rights reserved.

Printed in the United States of America.

Published by O'Reilly Media, Inc., 1005 Gravenstein Highway North, Sebastopol, CA 95472.

O'Reilly books may be purchased for educational, business, or sales promotional use. Online editions are also available for most titles (*http://safaribooksonline.com*). For more information, contact our corporate/institutional sales department: 800-998-9938 or corporate@oreilly.com.

Editor: Heather Scherer	**Interior Designer:** David Futato
Production Editor: Kristen Brown	**Cover Designer:** Ellie Volckhausen
Copyeditor: Phil Dangler	**Illustrator:** Rebecca Demarest

February 2015:   First Edition

Revision History for the First Edition

2015-02-20:   First Release

See *http://oreilly.com/catalog/errata.csp?isbn=9781491924228* for release details.

The O'Reilly logo is a registered trademark of O'Reilly Media, Inc. *Migrating to Cloud-Native Application Architectures*, the cover image, and related trade dress are trademarks of O'Reilly Media, Inc.

978-1-491-92679-6

[LSI]

Table of Contents

The Rise of Cloud-Native

Software is eating the world.

—Mark Andreessen

Stable industries that have for years been dominated by entrenched leaders are rapidly being disrupted, and they're being disrupted by businesses with software at their core. Companies like Square, Uber, Netflix, Airbnb, and Tesla continue to possess rapidly growing private market valuations and turn the heads of executives of their industries' historical leaders. What do these innovative companies have in common?

- Speed of innovation
- Always-available services
- Web scale
- Mobile-centric user experiences

Moving to the cloud is a natural evolution of focusing on software, and cloud-native application architectures are at the center of how these companies obtained their disruptive character. By cloud, we mean any computing environment in which computing, networking, and storage resources can be provisioned and released elastically in an on-demand, self-service manner. This definition includes both public cloud infrastructure (such as Amazon Web Services, Google Cloud, or Microsoft Azure) and private cloud infrastructure (such as VMware vSphere or OpenStack).

In this chapter we'll explain how cloud-native application architectures enable these innovative characteristics. Then we'll examine a few key aspects of cloud-native application architectures.

Why Cloud-Native Application Architectures?

First we'll examine the common motivations behind moving to cloud-native application architectures.

Speed

It's become clear that speed wins in the marketplace. Businesses that are able to innovate, experiment, and deliver software-based solutions quickly are outcompeting those that follow more traditional delivery models.

In the enterprise, the time it takes to provision new application environments and deploy new versions of software is typically measured in days, weeks, or months. This lack of speed severely limits the risk that can be taken on by any one release, because the cost of making and fixing a mistake is also measured on that same timescale.

Internet companies are often cited for their practice of deploying hundreds of times per day. Why are frequent deployments important? If you can deploy hundreds of times per day, you can recover from mistakes almost instantly. If you can recover from mistakes almost instantly, you can take on more risk. If you can take on more risk, you can try wild experiments—the results might turn into your next competitive advantage.

The elasticity and self-service nature of cloud-based infrastructure naturally lends itself to this way of working. Provisioning a new application environment by making a call to a cloud service API is faster than a form-based manual process by several orders of magnitude. Deploying code to that new environment via another API call adds more speed. Adding self-service and hooks to teams' continuous integration/build server environments adds even more speed. Eventually we can measure the answer to Lean guru Mary Poppendick's question, "How long would it take your organization to deploy a change that involves just one single line of code?" in minutes or seconds.

Imagine what your team…what your business…could do if you were able to move that fast!

Safety

It's not enough to go extremely fast. If you get in your car and push the pedal to the floor, eventually you're going to have a rather expensive (or deadly!) accident. Transportation modes such as aircraft and express bullet trains are built for speed and safety. Cloud-native application architectures balance the need to move rapidly with the needs of stability, availability, and durability. It's possible and essential to have both.

As we've already mentioned, cloud-native application architectures enable us to rapidly recover from mistakes. We're not talking about mistake prevention, which has been the focus of many expensive hours of process engineering in the enterprise. Big design up front, exhaustive documentation, architectural review boards, and lengthy regression testing cycles all fly in the face of the speed that we're seeking. Of course, all of these practices were created with good intentions. Unfortunately, none of them have provided consistently measurable improvements in the number of defects that make it into production.

So how do we go fast and safe?

Visibility

Our architectures must provide us with the tools necessary to see failure when it happens. We need the ability to *measure everything*, establish a profile for "what's normal," detect deviations from the norm (including absolute values and rate of change), and identify the components contributing to those deviations. Feature-rich metrics, monitoring, alerting, and data visualization frameworks and tools are at the heart of all cloud-native application architectures.

Fault isolation

In order to limit the risk associated with failure, we need to limit the scope of components or features that could be affected by a failure. If no one could purchase products from Amazon.com every time the recommendations engine went down, that would be disastrous. Monolithic application architectures often possess this type of failure mode. Cloud-native application architectures often employ microservices ("Microservices" on page 10). By composing systems from microservices, we can limit the scope of a failure in any one microservice to just that microservice, but only if combined with *fault tolerance*.

Fault tolerance

It's not enough to decompose a system into independently deployable components; we must also prevent a failure in one of those components from causing a cascading failure across its possibly many transitive dependencies. Mike Nygard described several fault tolerance patterns in his book *Release It!* (Pragmatic Programmers), the most popular being the *circuit breaker*. A software circuit breaker works very similarly to an electrical circuit breaker: it prevents cascading failure by opening the circuit between the component it protects and the remainder of the failing system. It also can provide a graceful fallback behavior, such as a default set of product recommendations, while the circuit is open. We'll discuss this pattern in detail in "Fault-Tolerance" on page 42.

Automated recovery

With visibility, fault isolation, and fault tolerance, we have the tools we need to identify failure, recover from failure, and provide a reasonable level of service to our customers while we're engaging in the process of identification and recovery. Some failures are easy to identify: they present the same easily detectable pattern every time they occur. Take the example of a service health check, which usually has a binary answer: healthy or unhealthy, up or down. Many times we'll take the same course of action every time we encounter failures like these. In the case of the failed health check, we'll often simply restart or redeploy the service in question. Cloud-native application architectures don't wait for manual intervention in these situations. Instead, they employ automated detection and recovery. In other words, they let a computer wear the pager instead of a human.

Scale

As demand increases, we must scale our capacity to service that demand. In the past we handled more demand by scaling vertically: we bought larger servers. We eventually accomplished our goals, but slowly and at great expense. This led to capacity planning based on peak usage forecasting. We asked "what's the most computing power this service will ever need?" and then purchased enough hardware to meet that number. Many times we'd get this wrong, and we'd still blow our available capacity during events like Black Friday. But more often we'd be saddled with tens or hundreds of servers with mostly idle CPU's, which resulted in poor utilization metrics.

Innovative companies dealt with this problem through two pioneering moves:

- Rather than continuing to buy larger servers, they horizontally scaled application instances across large numbers of cheaper commodity machines. These machines were easier to acquire (or assemble) and deploy quickly.

- Poor utilization of existing large servers was improved by virtualizing several smaller servers in the same footprint and deploying multiple isolated workloads to them.

As public cloud infrastructure like Amazon Web Services became available, these two moves converged. The virtualization effort was delegated to the cloud provider, and the consumer focused on horizontal scale of its applications across large numbers of cloud server instances. Recently another shift has happened with the move from virtual servers to containers as the unit of application deployment. We'll discuss containers in "Containerization" on page 26.

This shift to the cloud opened the door for more innovation, as companies no longer required large amounts of startup capital to deploy their software. Ongoing maintenance also required a lower capital investment, and provisioning via API not only improved the speed of initial deployment, but also maximized the speed with which we could respond to changes in demand.

Unfortunately all of these benefits come with a cost. Applications must be architected differently for horizontal rather than vertical scale. The elasticity of the cloud demands ephemerality. Not only must we be able to create new application instances quickly; we must also be able to dispose of them quickly and safely. This need is a question of *state management*: how does the disposable interact with the persistent? Traditional methods such as clustered sessions and shared filesystems employed in mostly vertical architectures do not scale very well.

Another hallmark of cloud-native application architectures is the externalization of state to in-memory data grids, caches, and persistent object stores, while keeping the application instance itself essentially *stateless*. Stateless applications can be quickly created and destroyed, as well as attached to and detached from external state managers, enhancing our ability to respond to changes in demand. Of course this also requires the external state managers themselves to be scalable. Most cloud infrastructure providers have recognized this necessity and provide a healthy menu of such services.

Mobile Applications and Client Diversity

In January 2014, mobile devices accounted for 55% of Internet usage in the United States. Gone are the days of implementing applications targeted at users working on computer terminals tethered to desks. Instead we must assume that our users are walking around with multicore supercomputers in their pockets. This has serious implications for our application architectures, as exponentially more users can interact with our systems anytime and anywhere.

Take the example of viewing a checking account balance. This task used to be accomplished by calling the bank's call center, taking a trip to an ATM location, or asking a teller at one of the bank's branch locations. These customer interaction models placed significant limits on the demand that could be placed on the bank's underlying software systems at any one time.

The move to online banking services caused an uptick in demand, but still didn't fundamentally change the interaction model. You still had to physically be at a computer terminal to interact with the system, which still limited the demand significantly. Only when we all began, as my colleague Andrew Clay Shafer often says, "walking around with supercomputers in our pockets," did we start to inflict pain on these systems. Now thousands of customers can interact with the bank's systems *anytime* and *anywhere*. One bank executive has said that on payday, customers will check their balances several times every few minutes. Legacy banking systems simply weren't architected to meet this kind of demand, while cloud-native application architectures are.

The huge diversity in mobile platforms has also placed demands on application architectures. At any time customers may want to interact with our systems from devices produced by multiple different vendors, running multiple different operating platforms, running multiple versions of the same operating platform, and from devices of different form factors (e.g., phones vs. tablets). Not only does this place various constraints on the mobile application developers, but also on the developers of backend services.

Mobile applications often have to interact with multiple legacy systems as well as multiple microservices in a cloud-native application architecture. These services cannot be designed to support the unique needs of each of the diverse mobile platforms used by our customers. Forcing the burden of integration of these diverse services on the mobile developer increases latency and network trips, leading to slow response times and high battery usage, ultimately leading to users *deleting your app*. Cloud-native application architectures also support the notion of mobile-first development through design patterns such as the *API Gateway*, which transfers the burden of service aggregation back to the server-side. We'll discuss the API Gateway pattern in "API Gateways/Edge Services" on page 47.

Defining Cloud-Native Architectures

Now we'll explore several key characteristics of cloud-native application architectures. We'll also look at how these characteristics address motivations we've already discussed.

Twelve-Factor Applications

The twelve-factor app (*http://12factor.net*) is a collection of patterns for cloud-native application architectures, originally developed by engineers at Heroku. The patterns describe an application archetype that optimizes for the "why" of cloud-native application architectures. They focus on speed, safety, and scale by emphasizing declarative configuration, stateless/shared-nothing processes that horizontally scale, and an overall loose coupling to the deployment environment. Cloud application platforms like Cloud Foundry, Heroku, and Amazon Elastic Beanstalk are optimized for deploying twelve-factor apps.

In the context of twelve-factor, *application* (or *app*) refers to a single deployable unit. Organizations will often refer to multiple collaborating deployables as an *application*. In this context, however, we will refer to these multiple collaborating deployables as a *distributed system*.

A twelve-factor app can be described in the following ways:

Codebase
Each deployable app is tracked as one codebase tracked in revision control. It may have many deployed instances across multiple environments.

Dependencies
An app explicitly declares and isolates dependencies via appropriate tooling (e.g., Maven, Bundler, NPM) rather than depending on implicitly realized dependencies in its deployment environment.

Config
Configuration, or anything that is likely to differ between deployment environments (e.g., development, staging, production) is injected via operating system-level environment variables.

Backing services
Backing services, such as databases or message brokers, are treated as attached resources and consumed identically across all environments.

Build, release, run
The stages of building a deployable app artifact, combining that artifact with configuration, and starting one or more processes from that artifact/configuration combination, are strictly separated.

Processes
The app executes as one or more stateless processes (e.g., master/workers) that share nothing. Any necessary state is externalized to backing services (cache, object store, etc.).

Port binding
The app is self-contained and exports any/all services via port binding (including HTTP).

Concurrency
Concurrency is usually accomplished by scaling out app processes horizontally (though processes may also multiplex work via internally managed threads if desired).

Disposability
> Robustness is maximized via processes that start up quickly and shut down gracefully. These aspects allow for rapid elastic scaling, deployment of changes, and recovery from crashes.

Dev/prod parity
> Continuous delivery and deployment are enabled by keeping development, staging, and production environments as similar as possible.

Logs
> Rather than managing logfiles, treat logs as event streams, allowing the execution environment to collect, aggregate, index, and analyze the events via centralized services.

Admin processes
> Administrative or managements tasks, such as database migrations, are executed as one-off processes in environments identical to the app's long-running processes.

These characteristics lend themselves well to deploying applications quickly, as they make few to no assumptions about the environments to which they'll be deployed. This lack of assumptions allows the underlying cloud platform to use a simple and consistent mechanism, easily automated, to provision new environments quickly and to deploy these apps to them. In this way, the twelve-factor application patterns enable us to optimize for speed.

These characteristics also lend themselves well to the idea of ephemerality, or applications that we can "throw away" with very little cost. The application environment itself is 100% disposable, as any application *state*, be it in-memory or persistent, is extracted to some backing service. This allows the application to be scaled up and down in a very simple and elastic manner that is easily automated. In most cases, the underlying platform simply copies the existing environment the desired number of times and starts the processes. Scaling down is accomplished by halting the running processes and deleting the environments, with no effort expended backing up or otherwise preserving the state of those environments. In this way, the twelve-factor application patterns enable us to optimize for scale.

Finally, the disposability of the applications enables the underlying platform to automatically recover from failure events very quickly.

Furthermore, the treatment of logs as event streams greatly enables visibility into the underlying behavior of the applications at runtime. The enforced parity between environments and the consistency of configuration mechanisms and backing service management enable cloud platforms to provide rich visibility into all aspects of the application's runtime fabric. In this way, the twelve-factor application patterns enable us to optimize for safety.

Microservices

Microservices represent the decomposition of monolithic business systems into independently deployable services that do "one thing well." That one thing usually represents a business capability, or the smallest, "atomic" unit of service that delivers business value.

Microservice architectures enable speed, safety, and scale in several ways:

- As we decouple the business domain into independently deployable bounded contexts of capabilities, we also decouple the associated change cycles. As long as the changes are restricted to a single bounded context, and the service continues to fulfill its existing contracts, those changes can be made and deployed independent of any coordination with the rest of the business. The result is enablement of more frequent and rapid deployments, allowing for a continuous flow of value.

- Development can be accelerated by scaling the development organization itself. It's very difficult to build software faster by adding more people due to the overhead of communication and coordination. Fred Brooks taught us years ago that adding more people to a late software project makes it later. However, rather than placing all of the developers in a single sandbox, we can create parallel work streams by building more sandboxes through bounded contexts.

- The new developers that we add to each sandbox can ramp up and become productive more rapidly due to the reduced cognitive load of learning the business domain and the existing code, and building relationships within a smaller team.

- Adoption of new technology can be accelerated. Large monolithic application architectures are typically associated with long-term commitments to technical stacks. These commitments exist to mitigate the risk of adopting new technology by simply not doing it. Technology adoption mistakes are more expensive in a monolithic architecture, as those mistakes can pollute the entire enterprise architecture. If we adopt new technology within the scope of a single monolith, we isolate and minimze the risk in much the same way that we isolate and minimize the risk of runtime failure.

- Microservices offer independent, efficient scaling of services. Monolithic architectures can scale, but require us to scale all components, not simply those that are under heavy load. Microservices can be scaled if and only if their associated load requires it.

Self-Service Agile Infrastructure

Teams developing cloud-native application architectures are typically responsible for their deployment and ongoing operations. Successful adopters of cloud-native applications have empowered teams with self-service platforms.

Just as we create business capability teams to build microservices for each bounded context, we also create a capability team responsible for providing a platform on which to deploy and operate these microservices ("The Platform Operations Team" on page 22).

The best of these platforms raise the primary abstraction layer for their consumers. With infrastructure as a service (IAAS) we asked the API to create virtual server instances, networks, and storage, and then applied various forms of configuration management and automation to enable our applications and supporting services to run. Platforms are now emerging that allow us to think in terms of applications and backing services.

Application code is simply "pushed" in the form of pre-built artifacts (perhaps those produced as part of a continuous delivery pipeline) or raw source code to a Git remote. The platform then builds the application artifact, constructs an application environment, deploys the application, and starts the necessary processes. Teams do not have to think about where their code is running or how it got there, as the platform takes care of these types of concerns transparently.

The same model is supported for backing services. Need a database? How about a message queue or a mail server? Simply ask the platform to provision one that fits your needs. Platforms now support a wide range of SQL/NoSQL data stores, message queues, search engines, caches, and other important backing services. These service instances can then be "bound" to your application, with necessary credentials automatically injected into your application's environment for it to consume. A great deal of messy and error-prone bespoke automation is thereby eliminated.

These platforms also often provide a wide array of additional operational capabilities:

- Automated and on-demand scaling of application instances
- Application health management
- Dynamic routing and load balancing of requests to and across application instances
- Aggregation of logs and metrics

This combination of tools ensures that capability teams are able to develop and operate services according to agile principles, again enabling speed, safety, and scale.

API-Based Collaboration

The sole mode of interaction between services in a cloud-native application architecture is via published and versioned APIs. These APIs are typically HTTP REST-style with JSON serialization, but can use other protocols and serialization formats.

Teams are able to deploy new functionality whenever there is a need, without synchronizing with other teams, provided that they do not break any existing API contracts. The primary interaction model for the self-service infrastructure platform is also an API, just as it is with the business services. Rather than submitting tickets to provision, scale, and maintain application infrastructure, those same requests are submitted to an API that automatically services the requests.

Contract compliance can be verified on both sides of a service-to-service interaction via consumer-driven contracts (*http://bit.ly/ fowler-consumer-driven-contract*). Service consumers are not allowed to gain access to private implementation details of their dependencies or directly access their dependencies' data stores. In fact, only one service is ever allowed to gain direct access to any data store. This forced decoupling directly supports the cloud-native goal of speed.

Antifragility

The concept of antifragility was introduced in Nassim Taleb's book *Antifragile* (Random House). If fragility is the quality of a system that gets weaker or breaks when subjected to stressors, then what is the opposite of that? Many would respond with the idea of robustness or resilience—things that don't break or get weaker when subjected to stressors. However, Taleb introduces the opposite of fragility as antifragility, or the quality of a system that gets stronger when subjected to stressors. What systems work that way? Consider the human immune system, which gets stronger when exposed to pathogens and weaker when quarantined. Can we build architectures that way? Adopters of cloud-native architectures have sought to build them. One example is the Netflix Simian Army project, with the famous submodule "Chaos Monkey," which injects random failures into production components with the goal of identifying and eliminating weaknesses in the architecture. By explicitly seeking out weaknesses in the application architecture, injecting failures, and forcing their remediation, the architecture naturally converges on a greater degree of safety over time.

Summary

In this chapter we've examined the common motivations for moving to cloud-native application architectures in terms of abilities that we want to provide to our business via software:

Speed
> The ability to innovate, experiment, and deliver value more quickly than our competitors.

Safety
> The ability to move rapidly but also maintain stability, availability, and durability.

Scale
> The ability to elastically respond to changes in demand.

Mobility
> The ability for our customers to interact with us seamlessly from any location, on any device, and at any time.

We've also examined the unique characteristics of cloud-native application architectures and how they can help us provide these abilities:

Twelve-factor applications
> A set of patterns that optimize application design for speed, safety, and scale.

Microservices
> An architecture pattern that helps us align our units of deployment with business capabilities, allowing each capability to move independently and autonomously, and in turn faster and safer.

Self-service agile infrastructure
> Cloud platforms that enable development teams to operate at an application and service abstraction level, providing infrastructure-level speed, safety, and scale.

API-based collaboration
> An architecture pattern that defines service-to-service interaction as automatically verifiable contracts, enabling speed and safety through simplified integration work.

Antifragility
> As we increase stress on the system via speed and scale, the system improves its ability to respond, increasing safety.

In the next chapter we'll examine a few of the changes that most enterprises will need to make in order to adopt cloud-native application architectures.

Changes Needed

All we are doing is looking at the timeline from the moment a customer gives us an order to the point when we collect the cash. And we are reducing that timeline by removing the nonvalue-added wastes.

—Taichi Ohno

Taichi Ohno is widely recognized as the Father of Lean Manufacturing. Although the *practices* of lean manufacturing often don't translate perfectly into the world of software development, the *principles* normally do. These principles can guide us well in seeking out the changes necessary for a typical enterprise IT organization to adopt cloud-native application architectures, and to embrace the cultural and organizational transformations that are part of this shift.

Cultural Change

A great deal of the changes necessary for enterprise IT shops to adopt cloud-native architectures will not be technical at all. They will be cultural and organizational changes that revolve around eliminating structures, processes, and activities that create waste. In this section we'll examine the necessary cultural shifts.

From Silos to DevOps

Enterprise IT has typically been organized into many of the following silos:

- Software development
- Quality assurance
- Database administration

- System administration
- IT operations
- Release management
- Project management

These silos were created in order to allow those that understand a given specialty to manage and direct those that perform the work of that specialty. These silos often have different management hierarchies, toolsets, communication styles, vocabularies, and incentive structures. These differences inspire very different paradigms of the purpose of enterprise IT and how that purpose should be accomplished.

An often cited example of these conflicting paradigms is the view of change possessed by the development and operations organizations. Development's mission is usually viewed as delivering additional value to the organization through the development of software features. These features, by their very nature, introduce change into the IT ecosystem. So development's mission can be described as "delivering change," and is very often incentivized around how much change it delivers.

Conversely, IT operations' mission can be described as that of "preventing change." How? IT operations is usually tasked with maintaining the desired levels of availability, resiliency, performance, and durability of IT systems. Therefore they are very often incentivized to maintain key perfomance indicators (KPIs) such as mean time between failures (MTBF) and mean time to recovery (MTTR). One of the primary risk factors associated with any of these measures is the introduction of any type of change into the system. So, rather than find ways to safely introduce development's desired changes into the IT ecosystem, the knee-jerk reaction is often to put processes in place that make change painful, and thereby reduce the rate of change.

These differing paradigms obviously lead to many additional suboptimal collaborations. Collaboration, communication, and simple handoff of work product becomes tedious and painful at best, and absolutely chaotic (even dangerous) at worst. Enterprise IT often tries to "fix" the situation by creating heavyweight processes driven by ticket-based systems and committee meetings. And the enterprise IT value stream slows to a crawl under the weight of all of the nonvalue-adding waste.

Environments like these are diametrically opposed to the cloud-native idea of speed. Specialized silos and process are often motivated by the desire to create a safe environment. However they usually offer very little additional safety, and in some cases, make things worse!

At its heart, DevOps represents the idea of tearing down these silos and building shared toolsets, vocabularies, and communication structures in service of a culture focused on a single goal: delivering value rapidly and safely. Incentive structures are then created that reinforce and award behaviors that lead the organization in the direction of that goal. Bureaucracy and process are replaced by trust and accountability.

In this new world, development and IT operations report to the same immediate leadership and collaborate to find practices that support both the continuous delivery of value and the desired levels of availability, resiliency, performance, and durability. Today these context-sensitive practices increasingly include the adoption of cloud-native application architectures that provide the technological support needed to accomplish the organization's new shared goals.

From Punctuated Equilibrium to Continuous Delivery

Enterprises have often adopted agile processes such as Scrum, but only as local optimizations within development teams.

As an industry we've actually become fairly successful in transitioning individual development teams to a more agile way of working. We can begin projects with an inception (*http://bit.ly/agile-inception*), write user stories, and carry out all the routines of agile development such as iteration planning meetings, daily standups, retrospectives, and customer showcase demos. The adventurous among us might even venture into engineering practices like pair programming and test-driven development. Continuous integration, which used to be a fairly radical concept, has now become a standard part of the enterprise software lexicon. In fact, I've been a part of several enterprise software teams that have established highly optimized "story to demo" cycles, with the result of each development iteration being enthusiastically accepted during a customer demo.

But then these teams would receive that dreaded question:

> When can we see these features in our production environment?

This question is the most difficult for us to answer, as it forces us to consider forces that are beyond our control:

- How long will it take for us to navigate the independent quality assurance process?
- When will we be able to join a production release train?
- Can we get IT operations to provision a production environment for us in time?

It's at this point that we realize we're embedded in what Dave West has called the *waterscrumfall* (*http://bit.ly/waterscrumfall*). Our team has moved on to embrace agile principles, but our organization has not. So, rather than each iteration resulting in a production deployment (this was the original intent behind the Agile Manifesto value of *working software*), the code is actually batched up to participate in a more traditional downstream release cycle.

This operating style has direct consequences. Rather than each iteration resulting in value delivered to the customer and valuable feedback pouring back into the development team, we continue a "punctuated equilibrium" style of delivery. Punctuated equilibrium actually short-circuits two of the key benefits of agile delivery:

- Customers will likely go several weeks without seeing new value in the software. They perceive that this new agile way of working is just "business as usual," and do not develop the promised increased trust relationship with the development team. Because they don't see a reliable delivery cadence, they revert to their old practices of piling as many requirements as possible into releases. Why? Because they have little confidence that any software delivery will happen soon, they want as much value as possible to be included when it finally does occur.
- Teams may go several weeks without real feedback. Demos are great, but any seasoned developer knows that the best feedback comes only after real users engage with production software. That feedback provides valuable course corrections that enable teams to "build the right thing." By delaying this feedback, the

likelihood that the wrong thing gets built only increases, along with the associated costly rework.

Gaining the benefits of cloud-native application architectures requires a shift to continuous delivery. Rather than punctuated equilibrium driven by a waterscrumfall organization, we embrace the principles of value from end to end. A useful model for envisioning such a lifecycle is the idea of "Concept to Cash" described by Mary and Tom Poppendieck in their book *Implementing Lean Software Development* (Addison-Wesley). This approach considers all of the activities necessary to carry a business idea from its conception to the point where it generates profit, and constructs a value stream aligning people and process toward the optimal achievement of that goal.

We technically support this way of working with the engineering practices of continuous delivery, where every iteration (in fact, every source code commit!) is proven to be deployable in an automated fashion. We construct deployment pipelines which automate every test which would prevent a production deployment should that test fail. The only remaining decision to make is a business decision: does it make good business sense to deploy the available new features now? We already know they work as advertised, so do we want to give them to our customers? And because the deployment pipeline is fully automated, the business is able to act on that decision with the click of a button.

Centralized Governance to Decentralized Autonomy

One portion of the waterscrumfall culture merits a special mention, as I have seen it become a real sticking point in cloud-native adoption.

Enterprises normally adopt centralized governance structures around application architecture and data management, with committees responsible for maintaining guidelines and standards, as well as approving individual designs and changes. Centralized governance is intended to help with a few issues:

- It can prevent widespread inconsistencies in technology stacks, decreasing the overall maintenance burden for the organization.

- It can prevent widespread inconsistencies in architectural choices, allowing for a common view of application development across the organization.

- Cross-cutting concerns like regulatory compliance can be handled in a consistent way for the entire organization.

- Ownership of data can be determined by those who have a broad view of all organizational concerns.

These structures are created with the belief that they will result in higher quality, lower costs, or both. However, these structures rarely result in the quality improvements or cost savings desired, and further prevent the speed of delivery sought from cloud-native application architectures. Just as monolithic application architectures can create bottlenecks which limit the speed of technical innovation, monolithic governance structures can do the same. Architectural committees often only assemble periodically, and long waiting queues of work often ensue. Even small data model changes—changes that could be implemented in minutes or hours, and that would be readily approved by the committee—lay wasting in an ever-growing stack of to-do items.

Adoption of cloud-native application architectures is almost always coupled with a move to decentralized governance. The teams building cloud-native applications ("Business Capability Teams" on page 21) own all facets of the capability they're charged with delivering. They own and govern the data, the technology stack, the application architecture, the design of individual components, and the API contract delivered to the remainder of the organization. If a decision needs to be made, it's made and executed upon autonomously by the team.

The decentralization and autonomy of individual teams is balanced by minimal, lightweight structures that are imposed on the integration patterns used between independently developed and deployed services (e.g., they prefer HTTP REST JSON APIs rather than many different styles of RPC). These structures often emerge through grassroots adoption of solutions to cross-cutting problems like fault tolerance. Teams are encouraged to devise solutions to these problems locally, and then self-organize with other teams to establish common patterns and frameworks. As a preferred solution for the entire organization emerges, ownership of that solution is very often transfered to a cloud frameworks/tools team, which may or may not be embedded in the platform operations team ("The Platform Operations Team" on page 22). This cloud frameworks/tools team will often pioneer solutions as well while the organization is reforming around a shared understanding of the architecture.

Organizational Change

In this section we'll examine the necessary changes to how organizations create teams when adopting cloud-native application architectures. The theory behind this reorganization is the famous observation known as *Conway's Law*. Our solution is to create a team combining staff with many disciplines around each long-term product, instead of segregating staff that have a single discipline in each own team, such as testing.

Business Capability Teams

> Any organization that designs a system (defined broadly) will produce a design whose structure is a copy of the organization's communication structure.
>
> —Melvyn Conway

We've already discussed in "From Silos to DevOps" on page 15 the practice of organizing IT into specialized silos. Quite naturally, having created these silos, we have also placed individuals into teams aligned with these silos. But what happens when we need to build a new piece of software?

A very common practice is to commission a project team. The team is assigned a project manager, and the project manager then collaborates with various silos to obtain "resources" for each specialty needed to staff the project. Part of what we learn from Conway's Law, quoted above, is that these teams will then very naturally produce in their system design the very silos from which they hail. And so we end up with siloed architectures having modules aligned with the silos themselves:

- Data access tier
- Services tier

- Web MVC tier
- Messaging tier
- Etc.

Each of these tiers spans multiple identifiable business capabilities, making it very difficult to innovate and deploy features related to one business capability independently from the others.

Companies seeking to move to cloud-native architectures like microservices segregated by business capability have often employed what Thoughtworks has called the Inverse Conway Maneuver (*http://bit.ly/inverse-conway*). Rather than building an architecture that matches their org chart, they determine the architecture they want and restructure their organization to match that architecture. If you do that, according to Conway, the architecture that you desire will eventually emerge.

So, as part of the shift to a DevOps culture, teams are organized as cross-functional, business capability teams that develop *products* rather than *projects*. Products are long-lived efforts that continue until they no longer provide value to the business. (You're done when your code is no longer in production!) All of the roles necessary to build, test, deliver, and operate the service delivering a business capability are present on a team, which doesn't hand off code to other parts of the organization. These teams are often organized as "two-pizza teams" (*http://bit.ly/bezos-interview*), meaning that the team is too big if it cannot be fed with two pizzas.

What remains then is to determine what teams to create. If we follow the Inverse Conway Maneuver, we'll start with the domain model for the organization, and seek to identify business capabilities that can be encapsulated within *bounded contexts* (which we'll cover in "Decomposing Data" on page 24). Once we identify these capabilities, we create business capability teams to own them throughout their useful lifecycle. Business capability teams own the entire development-to-operations lifecycle for their applications.

The Platform Operations Team

The business capability teams need to rely on the self-service agile infrastructure described earlier in "Self-Service Agile Infrastructure" on page 11. In fact, we can express a special business capability defined as "the ability to develop, deploy, and operate business capabilities." This capability is owned by the platform operations team.

The platform operations team operates the self-service agile infrastructure platform leveraged by the business capability teams. This team typically includes the traditional system, network, and storage administrator roles. If the company is operating the cloud platform on premises, this team also either owns or collaborates closely with teams managing the data centers themselves, and understands the hardware capabilities necessary to provide an infrastructure platform.

IT operations has traditionally interacted with its customers via a variety of ticket-based systems. Because the platform operations team operates a self-service platform, it must interact differently. Just as the business capability teams collaborate with one another around defined API contracts, the platform operations team presents an API contract for the platform. Rather than queuing up requests for application environments and data services to be provisioned, business capability teams are able to take the leaner approach of building automated release pipelines that provision environments and services on-demand.

Technical Change

Now we can turn to some implementation issues in moving to a DevOps platform in the cloud.

Decomposing Monoliths

Traditional *n*-tier, monolithic enterprise applications rarely operate well when deployed to cloud infrastructure, as they often make unsupportable assumptions about their deployment environment that cloud infrastructures simply cannot provide. A few examples include:

- Access to mounted, shared filesystems
- Peer-to-peer application server clustering
- Shared libraries
- Configuration files sitting in well-known locations

Most of these assumptions are coupled with the fact that monoliths are typically deployed to long-lived infrastructure. Unfortunately, they are not very compatible with the idea of elastic and ephemeral infrastructure.

But let's assume that we could build a monolith that does not make any of these assumptions. We still have trouble:

- Monoliths couple change cycles together such that independent business capabilities cannot be deployed as required, preventing speed of innovation.

- Services embedded in monoliths cannot be scaled independently of other services, so load is far more difficult to account for efficiently.

- Developers new to the organization must acclimate to a new team, often learn a new business domain, and become familiar with an extremely large codebase all at once. This only adds to the typical 3–6 month ramp up time before achieving real productivity.

- Attempting to scale the development organization by adding more people further crowds the sandbox, adding expensive coordination and communication overhead.

- Technical stacks are committed to for the long term. Introducing new technology is considered too risky, as it can adversely affect the entire monolith.

The observant reader will notice that this list is the inverse of the list from "Microservices" on page 10. The decomposition of the organization into business capability teams also requires that we decompose applications into microservices. Only then can we harness the maximum benefit from our move to cloud infrastructure.

Decomposing Data

It's not enough to decompose monolithic applications into microservices. Data models must also be decoupled. If business capability teams are supposedly autonomous but are forced to collaborate via a single data store, the monolithic barrier to innovation is simply relocated.

In fact, it's arguable that product architecture must start with the data. The principles found in *Domain-Driven Design (DDD)*, by Eric

Evans (Addison-Wesley), argue that our success is largely governed by the quality of our domain model (and the ubiquitous language that underpins it). For a domain model to be effective, it must also be internally consistent—we should not find terms or concepts with inconsistent definitions within the same model.

It is incredibly difficult and costly (and arguably impossible) to create a federated domain model that does not suffer from such inconsistencies. Evans refers to internally consistent subsets of the overall domain model of the business as *bounded contexts*.

When working with an airline customer recently, we were discussing the concepts most central to their business. Naturally the topic of "airline reservation" came up. The group could count *seventeen* different logical definitions of reservation within its business, with little to no hope of reconciling them into one. Instead, all of the nuance of each definition was carefully baked into a single concept, which became a huge bottleneck for the organization.

Bounded contexts allow you to keep inconsistent definitions of a single concept across the organization, as long as they are defined consistently within the contexts themselves.

So we begin by identifying the segments of the domain model that can be made internally consistent. We draw fixed boundaries around these segments, which become our bounded contexts. We're then able to align business capability teams with these contexts, and those teams build microservices providing those capabilities.

This definition of microservice provides a useful rubric for defining what your twelve-factor apps ought to be. Twelve-factor is primarily a technical specification, whereas microservices are primarily a business specification. We define our bounded contexts, assign them a set of business capabilities, commission capability teams to own those business capabilities, and have them build twelve-factor applications. The fact that these applications are independently deployable provides business capability teams with a useful set of technical tools for operation.

We couple bounded contexts with the *database per service* pattern, where each microservice encapsulates, governs, and protects its own domain model and persistent store. In the database per service pattern, only one application service is allowed to gain access to a logical data store, which could exist as a single schema within a multi-tenant cluster or a dedicated physical database. Any external access to the concepts is made through a well-defined business contract implemented as an API (often REST but potentially any protocol).

This decomposition allows for the application of polyglot persistence, or choosing different data stores based on data shape and read/write access patterns. However, data must often be recomposed via event-driven techniques in order to ask cross-context questions. Techniques such as *command query responsibility segregation* (CQRS) (*http://bit.ly/fowler-cqrs*) and *event sourcing* (*http://bit.ly/fowler-es*), beyond the scope of this report, are often helpful when synchronizing similar concepts across contexts.

Containerization

Container images, such as those prepared via the LXC (*https://linux containers.org/*), Docker (*https://www.docker.com/*), or Rocket (*https://github.com/coreos/rocket*) projects, are rapidly becoming the unit of deployment for cloud-native application architectures. Such container images are then instantiated by various scheduling solutions such as Kubernetes, Marathon, or Lattice. Public cloud providers such as Amazon and Google also provide first-class solutions for container scheduling and deployment. Containers leverage modern Linux kernel primitives such as control groups (cgroups) and namespaces to provide similar resource allocation and isolation features as those provided by virtual machines with much less overhead and much greater portability. Application developers will need to become comfortable packaging applications as container images to take full advantage of the features of modern cloud infrastructure.

From Orchestration to Choreography

Not only must service delivery, data modeling, and governance be decentralized, but also service integration. Enterprise integration of services has traditionally been accomplished via the *enterprise service bus* (ESB). The ESB becomes the owner of all routing, transformation, policy, security, and other decisions governing the interaction between services. We call this *orchestration*, analogous to the conductor who determines the course of the music performed by an orchestra during its performance. ESBs and orchestration make for very simple and pleasing architecture diagrams, but their simplicity is deceiving. Often hiding within the ESB is a tangled web of complexity. Managing this complexity becomes a full-time occupation, and working with it becomes a continual bottleneck for the application development team. Just as we saw with a federated data model, a federated integration solution like the ESB becomes a monolithic hazard to speed.

Cloud-native architectures, such as microservices, tend to prefer *choreography*, akin to dancers in a ballet. Rather than placing the smarts in the integration mechanism, they are placed in the endpoints, akin to the dumb pipes and smart filters of the Unix architecture. When circumstances on stage differ from the original plan, there's no conductor present to tell the dancers what to do. Instead, they simply adapt. In the same way, services adapt to changing circumstances in their environment via patterns such as client-side load balancing ("Routing and Load Balancing" on page 39) and circuit breakers ("Fault-Tolerance" on page 42).

While the architecture diagrams tend to look like a tangled web, their complexity is no greater than a traditional SOA. Choreography simply acknowledges and exposes the essential complexity of the system. Once again this shift is in support of the autonomy required to enable the speed sought from cloud-native architectures. Teams are able to adapt to their changing circumstances without the difficult overhead of coordinating with other teams, and avoid the overhead of coordinating changes with a centrally-managed ESB.

Summary

In this chapter we've examined a few of the changes that most enterprises will need to make in order to adopt cloud-native application architectures. Culturally the overall theme is one of decentralization and autonomy:

DevOps
Decentralization of skill sets into cross-functional teams.

Continuous delivery
Decentralization of the release schedule and process.

Autonomy
Decentralization of decision making.

We codify this decentralization into two primary team structures:

Business capability teams
> Cross-functional teams that make their own decisions about design, process, and release schedule.

Platform operations teams
> Teams that provide the cross-functional teams with the platform they need to operate.

And technically, we also decentralize control:

Monoliths to microservices
> Control of individual business capabilities is distributed to individual autonomous services.

Bounded contexts
> Control of internally consistent subsets of the business domain model is distributed to microservices.

Containerization
> Control of application packaging is distributed to business capability teams.

Choreography
> Control of service integration is distributed to the service endpoints.

All of these changes create autonomous units that are able to safely move at the desired rate of innovation.

In the final chapter, we'll delve into technical specifics of migrating to cloud-native application architectures through a set of cookbook-style recipes.

Migration Cookbook

Now that we've defined cloud-native application architectures and given a brief high-level overview of the changes enterprises must consider when adopting them, it's time to delve into technical specifics. Each of these topics minimally merits its own chapter, and that's beyond the scope of this report. Instead, this chapter provides a set of short, cookbook-style recipes to help with specific tasks and patterns needed to adopt a cloud-native application architecture, along with links to helpful further reading.

Decomposition Recipes

After discussing the decomposition of data, services, and teams with customers, I'm often asked, "Great! How do we get there from here?" Good question. How do we tear apart existing monoliths and move them to the cloud?

As it turns out, I've seen companies succeed with a fairly repeatable pattern of incremental migration which I now recommend to all of my customers. Publicly referenceable examples (*http://bit.ly/sc-monolith-1*) of this pattern can be found at SoundCloud (*http://bit.ly/sc-monolith-2*) and Karma (*http://bit.ly/karma-build-micro*).

In this section we'll walk step-by-step through a series of recipes that provide a process for decomposing monolithic services and moving them to the cloud.

New Features as Microservices

Surprisingly, the first step is not to start chipping away at the monolith itself. We'll begin with the assumption that you still have a backlog of features to be built within the monolith. In fact, if you *don't* have any net new functionality to build, it's arguable that you shouldn't even be considering this decomposition. (Given that our primary motivation is speed, how do you leave something unchanged really fast?)

> ...the team decided that the best approach to deal with the architecture changes would not be to split the Mothership immediately, but rather to not add anything new to it. All of our new features were built as microservices...
>
> —Phil Calcado, SoundCloud

So it's time to stop adding new code to the monolith. All new features will be built as microservices. Get good at this first, as building new services from scratch is far easier than surgically extracting them from a big ball of mud (*http://www.laputan.org/mud/*).

Inevitably, however, these new microservices will need to talk back to the monolith in order to get anything done. How do we attack that problem?

The Anti-Corruption Layer

> Because so much of our logic was still in the Rails monolith, pretty much all of our microservices had to talk to it somehow.
>
> —Phil Calcado, SoundCloud

Domain-Driven Design (DDD), by Eric Evans (Addison-Wesley), discusses the idea of an *anti-corruption layer*. Its purpose is to allow the integration of two systems without allowing the domain model of one system to corrupt the domain model of the other. As you build new functionality into microservices, you don't want these new services to become tightly coupled with the monolith by giving them deep knowledge of the monolith's internals. The anti-corruption layer is a way of creating API contracts that make the monolith look like other microservices.

Evans divides the implementation of anti-corruption layers into three submodules, the first two representing classic design patterns (from Gamma et al., *Design Patterns: Elements of Reusable Object-Oriented Software* [Addison Wesley]):

Facade

> The purpose of the facade module here is to simplify the process of integrating with the monolith's interface. It's very likely that the monolith was not designed with this type of integration in mind, so the facade's purpose is to solve this problem. Importantly, it does not change the monolith's model, being careful not to couple translation and integration concerns.

Adapter

> The adapter is where we define "services" that provide things our new features need. It knows how to take a request from our system, using a protocol that it understands, and make that request to the monolith's facade(s).

Translator

> The translator's responsibility is to convert requests and responses between the domain model of the monolith and the domain model of the new microservice.

These three loosely coupled components solve three problems:

1. System integration
2. Protocol translation
3. Model translation

What remains is the location of the communication link. In *DDD*, Evans discusses two alternatives. The first, *facade to system*, is primarily useful when you can't access or alter the legacy system. Our focus here is on monoliths we do control, so we'll lean toward Evans' second suggestion, *adapter to facade*. Using this alternative, we build the facade into the monolith, allowing communications to occur between the adapter and the facade, as presumably it's easier to create this link between two things written explicitly for this purpose.

Finally, it's important to note that anti-corruption layers can facilitate two-way communication. Just as our new microservices may need to communicate with the monolith to accomplish work, the inverse may be true as well, particularly as we move on to our next phase.

Strangling the Monolith

> After the architecture changes were made, our teams were free to
> build their new features and enhancements in a much more flexible
> environment. An important question remained, though: how do we
> extract the features from the monolithic Rails application called
> Mothership?
>
> —Phil Calcado, SoundCloud

I borrow the idea of "strangling the monolith" from Martin Fowler's
article entitled "StranglerApplication" (*http://bit.ly/stranglerapp*). In
this article, Fowler explains the idea of gradually creating "a new system around the edges of the old, letting it grow slowly over several
years until the old system is strangled." We're effectively going to do
the same thing here. Through a combination of extracted microservices and additional anti-corruption layers, we'll build a new cloud-
native system around the edges of the existing monolith.

Two criteria help us choose which components to extract:

1. SoundCloud nails the first criterion: identify bounded contexts
   within the monolith. If you'll recall our earlier discussions of
   bounded contexts, they require a domain model that is internally consistent. It's extremely likely that our monolith's domain
   model is not internally consistent. Now it's time to start identifying submodels that can be. These are our candidates for
   extraction.

2. Our second criterion deals with priority: which of our candidates do we extract first? We can answer this by reviewing our
   first reason for moving to cloud-native architecture: speed of
   innovation. What candidate microservices will benefit most
   from speed of innovation? We obviously want to choose those
   that are changing the most given our current business needs.
   Look at the monolith's backlog. Identify the areas of the monolith's code that will need to change in order to deliver the
   changed requirements, and then extract the appropriate bounded contexts before making the desired changes.

Potential End States

How do we know when we are finished? There are basically two end states:

1. The monolith has been completely strangled to death. All bounded contexts have been extracted into microservices. The final step is to identify opportunities to eliminate anti-corruption layers that are no longer necessary.

2. The monolith has been strangled to a point where the cost of additional service extraction exceeds the return on the necessary development efforts. Some portions of the monolith may be fairly stable—we haven't changed them in years and they're doing their jobs. There may not be much value in moving these portions around, and the cost of maintaining the necessary anti-corruption layers to integrate with them may be low enough that we can take it on long-term.

Distributed Systems Recipes

As we start to build distributed systems composed from microservices, we'll also encounter nonfunctional requirements that we don't normally encounter when developing a monolith. Sometimes the laws of physics get in the way of solving these problems, such as consistency, latency, and network partitions. However, the problems of brittleness and manageability can normally be addressed through the proper application of fairly generic, boilerplate patterns. In this section we'll examine recipes that help us with these concerns.

These recipes are drawn from a combination of the Spring Cloud (*http://bit.ly/spring-cloud*) project and the Netflix OSS (*http://netflix.github.io*) family of projects.

Versioned and Distributed Configuration

We discussed the importance of proper configuration management for applications in "Twelve-Factor Applications" on page 7, which specifies the injection of configuration via operating system-level environment variables. This method is very suitable for simple systems, but as we scale up to larger systems, sometimes we want additional configuration capabilities:

- Changing logging levels of a running application in order to debug a production issue
- Change the number of threads receiving messages from a message broker
- Report all configuration changes made to a production system to support regulatory audits
- Toggle features on/off in a running application
- Protect secrets (such as passwords) embedded in configuration

In order to support these capabilities, we need a configuration management approach with the following features:

- Versioning
- Auditability
- Encryption
- Refresh without restart

The Spring Cloud project contains a Config Server (*http://bit.ly/ spring-config*) that provides these features. This Config Server presents application and application profile (e.g., sets of configuration that can be toggled on/off as a set, such as a "development" or "staging" profile) configuration as a REST API backed by a Git repository (Figure 3-1).

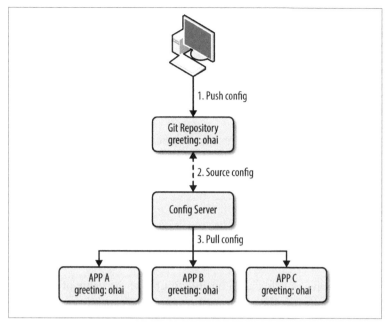

Figure 3-1. The Spring Cloud Config Server

As an example, here's the default application profile configuration for a sample Config Server (Example 3-1).

Example 3-1. Default application profile configuration for a sample Config Server

```
{
    "label": "",
    "name": "default",
    "propertySources": [
      {
          "name": "https://github.com/mstine/config-repo.git/applica
tion.yml", ❶
          "source": {
            "greeting": "ohai" ❷
          }
      }
    ]
}
```

❶ This configuration is backed by the file `application.yml` in the specified backing Git repository.

❷ The `greeting` is currently set to `ohai`.

The configuration in Example 3-1 was not manually coded, but generated automatically. We can see that the value for `greeting` is being distributed to the Spring application by examining its `/env` endpoint (Example 3-2).

Example 3-2. Environment for a Config Server client

```
"configService:https://github.com/mstine/config-repo.git/applica
tion.yml": {
  "greeting": "ohai" ❶
},
```

❶ This application is receiving its `greeting` value of `ohai` from the Config Server.

All that remains is for us to be able to update the value of `greeting` without restarting the client application. This capability is provided by another Spring Cloud project module called Spring Cloud Bus (*http://bit.ly/spring-bus*). This project links nodes of a distributed system with a lightweight message broker, which can then be used to broadcast state changes such as our desired configuration change (Figure 3-2).

Simply by performing an HTTP POST to the `/bus/refresh` endpoint of any application participating in the bus (which should obviously be guarded with appropriate security), we can instruct all applications on the bus to refresh their configuration with the latest available values from the Config Server.

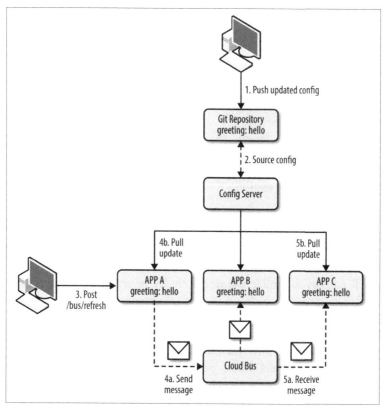

Figure 3-2. The Spring Cloud Bus

Service Registration/Discovery

As we create distributed systems, our code's dependencies cease to be a method call away. Instead, we must make network calls in order to consume them. How do we perform the necessary wiring to allow all of the microservices within a composed system to communicate with one another?

A common architecture pattern in the cloud (Figure 3-3) is to have frontend (application) and backend (business) services. Backend services are often not accessible directly from the Internet but are rather accessed via the frontend services. The service registry provides a listing of all services and makes them available to frontend services through a client library ("Routing and Load Balancing" on page 39) which performs load balancing and routing to backend services.

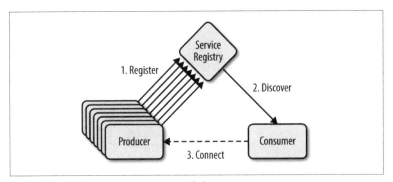

Figure 3-3. Service registration and discovery

We've solved this problem before using various incarnations of the Service Locator (*http://bit.ly/service-locator*) and Dependency Injection (*http://bit.ly/dependency-inject*) patterns, and service-oriented architectures have long employed various forms of service registries. We'll employ a similar solution here by leveraging Eureka (*http://bit.ly/net-eureka*), which is a Netflix OSS project that can be used for locating services for the purpose of load balancing and failover of middle-tier services. Consumption of Eureka is further simplified for Spring applications via the Spring Cloud Netflix (*http://bit.ly/spring-netflix*) project, which provides a primarily annotation-based configuration model for consuming Netflix OSS services.

An application leveraging Spring Boot (*http://bit.ly/spring-boot*) can participate in service registration and discovery simply by adding the @EnableDiscoveryClient annotation (Example 3-3).

Example 3-3. A Spring Boot application with service registration/ discovery enabled

```
@SpringBootApplication
@EnableDiscoveryClient ❶
public class Application {

  public static void main(String[] args) {
    SpringApplication.run(Application.class, args);
  }

}
```

❶ The @EnableDiscoveryClient enables service registration/ discovery for this application.

The application is then able to communicate with its dependencies by leveraging the DiscoveryClient. In Example 3-4, the application looks up an instance of a service registered with the name PRODUCER, obtains its URL, and then leverages Spring's RestTemplate to communicate with it.

Example 3-4. Using the DiscoveryClient to locate a producer service

```
@Autowired
DiscoveryClient discoveryClient; ❶

@RequestMapping("/")
public String consume() {
    InstanceInfo instance = discoveryClient.getNextServerFromEur
eka("PRODUCER", false); ❷

  RestTemplate restTemplate = new RestTemplate();
      ProducerResponse    response    =    restTemplate.getForOb
ject(instance.getHomePageUrl(), ProducerResponse.class);

  return "{\"value\": \"" + response.getValue() + "\"}";
}
```

❶ The enabled DiscoveryClient is injected by Spring.

❷ The getNextServerFromEureka method provides the location of a service instance using a round-robin algorithm.

Routing and Load Balancing

Basic round-robin load balancing is effective for many scenarios, but distributed systems in cloud environments often demand a more advanced set of routing and load balancing behaviors. These are commonly provided by various external, centralized load balancing solutions. However, it's often true that such solutions do not possess enough information or context to make the best choices for a given application as it attempts to communicate with its dependencies. Also, should such external solutions fail, these failures can cascade across the entire architecture.

Cloud-native solutions often often shift the responsibility for making routing and load balancing solutions to the client. One such client-side solution is the Ribbon (*http://bit.ly/ribbon-netflix*) Netflix OSS project (Figure 3-4).

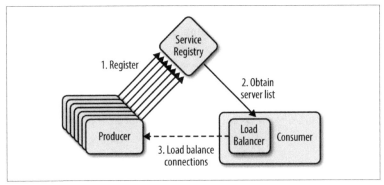

Figure 3-4. Ribbon client-side load balancer

Ribbon provides a rich set of features including:

- Multiple built-in load balancing rules:
  — Round-robin
  — Average response-time weighted
  — Random
  — Availability filtered (avoid tripped circuits or high concurrent connection counts)
- Custom load balancing rule plugin system
- Pluggable integration with service discovery solutions (including Eureka)
- Cloud-native intelligence such as zone affinity and unhealthy zone avoidance
- Built-in failure resiliency

As with Eureka, the Spring Cloud Netflix (*http://bit.ly/spring-netflix*) project greatly simplifies a Spring application developer's consumption of Ribbon. Rather than injecting an instance of `Discovery Client` (for direct consumption of Eureka), developers can inject an instance of `LoadBalancerClient`, and then use that to resolve an instance of the application's dependencies (Example 3-5).

Example 3-5. Using the `LoadBalancerClient` to locate a producer service

```
@Autowired
LoadBalancerClient loadBalancer; ❶
```

```
@RequestMapping("/")
public String consume() {
  ServiceInstance instance = loadBalancer.choose("producer"); ❷
    URI    producerUri   =   URI.create("http://${instance.host}:$
{instance.port}");

  RestTemplate restTemplate = new RestTemplate();
   ProducerResponse response = restTemplate.getForObject(producer
Uri, ProducerResponse.class);

  return "{\"value\": \"" + response.getValue() + "\"}";
}
```

❶   The enabled `LoadBalancerClient` is injected by Spring.

❷   The `choose` method provides the location of a service instance using the currently enabled load balancing algorithm.

Spring Cloud Netflix further simplifies the consumption of Ribbon by creating a Ribbon-enabled `RestTemplate` bean which can be injected into beans. This instance of `RestTemplate` is configured to automatically resolve instances of logical service names to instance URIs using Ribbon (Example 3-6).

Example 3-6. Using the Ribbon-enabled RestTemplate

```
@Autowired
RestTemplate restTemplate; ❶

@RequestMapping("/")
public String consume() {
   ProducerResponse response = restTemplate.getForObject("http://
producer", ProducerResponse.class); ❷
  return "{\"value\": \"" + response.getValue() + "\"}";
}
```

❶   `RestTemplate` is injected rather than a `LoadBalancerClient`.

❷   The injected `RestTemplate` automatically resolves `http://producer` to an actual service instance URI.

Fault-Tolerance

Distributed systems have more potential failure modes than monoliths. As each incoming request must now potentially touch tens (or even hundreds) of different microservices, some failure in one or more of those dependencies is virtually guaranteed.

> Without taking steps to ensure fault tolerance, 30 dependencies each with 99.99% uptime would result in 2+ hours downtime/month (99.99%^30^ = 99.7% uptime = 2+ hours in a month).
>
> —Ben Christensen,
> Netflix Engineer

How do we prevent such failures from resulting in the type of cascading failures that would give us such negative availability numbers (*http://bit.ly/netflix-fault-tol*)? Mike Nygard documented several patterns that can help in his book *Release It!* (Pragmatic Programmers), including:

Circuit breakers

Circuit breakers insulate a service from its dependencies by preventing remote calls when a dependency is determined to be unhealthy, just as electrical circuit breakers protect homes from burning down due to excessive use of power. Circuit breakers are implemented as state machines (Figure 3-5). When in their closed state, calls are simply passed through to the dependency. If any of these calls fails, the failure is counted. When the failure count reaches a specified threshold within a specified time period, the circuit trips into the open state. In the open state, calls always fail immediately. After a predetermined period of time, the circuit transitions into a "half-open" state. In this state, calls are again attempted to the remote dependency. Successful calls transition the circuit breaker back into the closed state, while failed calls return the circuit breaker to the open state.

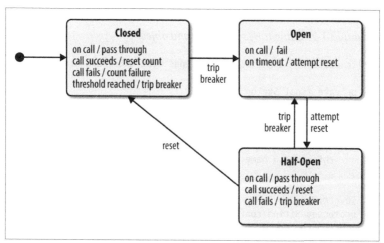

Figure 3-5. A circuit breaker state machine

Bulkheads

Bulkheads partition a service in order to confine errors and prevent the entire service from failing due to failure in one area. They are named for partitions that can be sealed to segment a ship into multiple watertight compartments. This can prevent damage (e.g., caused by a torpedo hit) from causing the entire ship to sink. Software systems can utilize bulkheads in many ways. Simply partitioning into microservices is our first line of defense. The partitioning of application processes into Linux containers ("Containerization" on page 26) so that one process cannot takeover an entire machine is another. Yet another example is the division of parallelized work into different thread pools.

Netflix has produced a very powerful library for fault tolerance in Hystrix (*http://bit.ly/hystrix*) that employs these patterns and more. Hystrix allows code to be wrapped in `HystrixCommand` objects in order to wrap that code in a circuit breaker.

Example 3-7. Using a `HystrixCommand` object

```
public class CommandHelloWorld extends HystrixCommand<String> {

    private final String name;

    public CommandHelloWorld(String name) {
                super(HystrixCommandGroupKey.Factory.asKey("Exam
pleGroup"));
        this.name = name;
    }

    @Override
    protected String run() { ❶
        return "Hello " + name + "!";
    }
}
```

❶   The code in the `run` method is wrapped with a circuit breaker

Spring Cloud Netflix adds an `@EnableCircuitBreaker` annotation to enable the Hystrix runtime components in a Spring Boot application. It then leverages a set of contributed annotations (*http://bit.ly/ histrix-contrib*) to make programming with Spring and Hystrix as easy as the earlier integrations we've described (Example 3-8).

Example 3-8. Using @`HystrixCommand`

```
@Autowired
RestTemplate restTemplate;

@HystrixCommand(fallbackMethod = "getProducerFallback") ❶
public ProducerResponse getProducerResponse() {
    return restTemplate.getForObject("http://producer", ProducerRes
ponse.class);
}

public ProducerResponse getProducerFallback() { ❷
    return new ProducerResponse(42);
}
```

❶   The method annotated with @HystrixCommand is wrapped with a circuit breaker.

❷ The method `getProducerFallback` is referenced within the annotation and provides a graceful fallback behavior while the circuit is in the open or half-open state.

Hystrix is unique from many other circuit breaker implementations in that it also employs bulkheads by operating each circuit breaker within its own thread pool. It also collects many useful metrics about the circuit breaker's state, including:

- Traffic volume
- Request rate
- Error percentage
- Hosts reporting
- Latency percentiles
- Successes, failures, and rejections

These metrics are emitted as an event stream which can be aggregated by another Netflix OSS project called Turbine (*http://bit.ly/netflix-turbine*). Individual or aggregated metric streams can then be visualized using a powerful Hystrix Dashboard (Figure 3-6), providing excellent visibility into the overall health of the distributed system.

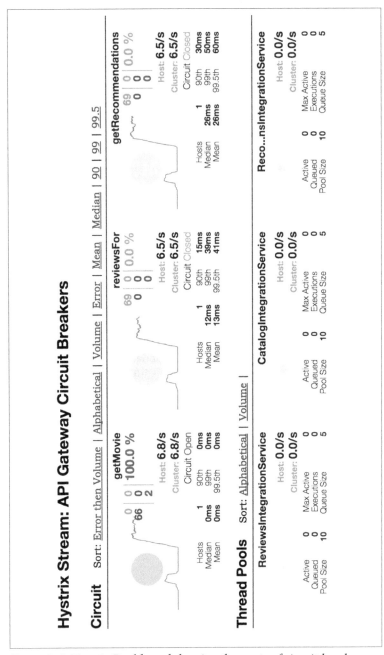

Figure 3-6. Hystrix Dashboard showing three sets of circuit breaker metrics

API Gateways/Edge Services

In "Mobile Applications and Client Diversity" on page 6 we discussed the idea of server-side aggregation and transformation of an ecosystem of microservices. Why is this necessary?

Latency

Mobile devices typically operate on lower speed networks than our in-home devices. The need to connect to tens (or hundreds?) of microservices in order to satisfy the needs of a single application screen would reduce latency to unacceptable levels even on our in-home or business networks. The need for concurrent access to these services quickly becomes clear. It is less expensive and error-prone to capture and implement these concurrent patterns once on the server-side than it is to do the same on each device platform.

A further source of latency is response size. Web service development has trended toward the "return everything you might possibly need" approach in recent years, resulting in much larger response payloads than is necessary to satisfy the needs of a single mobile device screen. Mobile device developers would prefer to reduce that latency by retrieving only the necessary information and ignoring the remainder.

Round trips

Even if network speed was not an issue, communicating with a large number of microservices would still cause problems for mobile developers. Network usage is one of the primary consumers of battery life on such devices. Mobile developers try to economize on network usage by making the fewest server-side calls possible to deliver the desired user experience.

Device diversity

The diversity within the mobile device ecosystem is enormous. Businesses must cope with a growing list of differences across their customer bases, including different:

- Manufacturers
- Device types
- Form factors
- Device sizes
- Programming languages

- Operating systems
- Runtime environments
- Concurrency models
- Supported network protocols

This diversity expands beyond even the mobile device ecosystem, as developers are now targeting a growing ecosystem of in-home consumer devices including smart televisions and set-top boxes.

The API Gateway (*http://bit.ly/api-gateway*) pattern (Figure 3-7) is targeted at shifting the burden of these requirements from the device developer to the server-side. API gateways are simply a special class of microservices that meet the needs of a single client application (such as a specific iPhone app), and provide it with a single entry point to the backend. They access tens (or hundreds) of microservices concurrently with each request, aggregating the responses and transforming them to meet the client application's needs. They also perform protocol translation (e.g., HTTP to AMQP) when necessary.

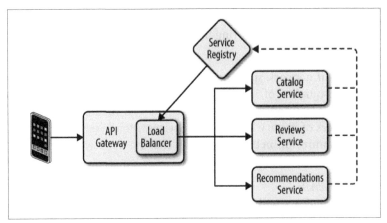

Figure 3-7. The API Gateway pattern

API gateways can be implemented using any language, runtime, or framework that well supports web programming, concurrency patterns, and the protocols necesssary to communicate with the target microservices. Popular choices include Node.js (due to its reactive programming model) and the Go programming language (due to its simple concurrency model).

In this discussion we'll stick with Java and give an example from RxJava (*http://bit.ly/rxjava-git*), a JVM implementation of Reactive Extensions (*http://reactivex.io/*) born at Netflix. Composing multiple work or data streams concurrently can be a challenge using only the primitives offered by the Java language, and RxJava is among a family of technologies (also including Reactor (*http://reactor.github.io/*)) targeted at relieving this complexity.

In this example we're building a Netflix-like site that presents users with a catalog of movies and the ability to create ratings and reviews for those movies. Further, when viewing a specific title, it provides recommendations to the viewer of movies they might like to watch if they like the title currently being viewed. In order to provide these capabilities, three microservices were developed:

- A catalog service
- A reviews service
- A recommendations service

The mobile application for this service expects a response like that found in Example 3-9.

Example 3-9. The movie details response

```
{
    "mlId": "1",
    "recommendations": [
        {
            "mlId": "2",
            "title": "GoldenEye (1995)"
        }
    ],
    "reviews": [
        {
            "mlId": "1",
            "rating": 5,
            "review": "Great movie!",
            "title": "Toy Story (1995)",
            "userName": "mstine"
        }
    ],
    "title": "Toy Story (1995)"
}
```

The code found in Example 3-10 utilizes RxJava's `Observable.zip` method to concurrently access each of the services. After receiving the three responses, the code passes them to the Java 8 Lambda that uses them to create an instance of `MovieDetails`. This instance of `MovieDetails` can then be serialized to produce the response found in Example 3-9.

Example 3-10. Concurrently accessing three services and aggregating their responses

```
Observable<MovieDetails> details = Observable.zip(

  catalogIntegrationService.getMovie(mlId),
  reviewsIntegrationService.reviewsFor(mlId),
  recommendationsIntegrationService.getRecommendations(mlId),

  (movie, reviews, recommendations) -> {
    MovieDetails movieDetails = new MovieDetails();
    movieDetails.setMlId(movie.getMlId());
    movieDetails.setTitle(movie.getTitle());
    movieDetails.setReviews(reviews);
    movieDetails.setRecommendations(recommendations);
    return movieDetails;
  }
);
```

This example barely scratches the surface of the available functionality in RxJava, and the reader is invited to explore the library further at RxJava's wiki (*http://bit.ly/rxjava-wiki*).

Summary

In this chapter we walked through two sets of recipes that can help us move toward a cloud-native application architecture:

Decomposition
We break down monolithic applications by:

1. Building all new features as microservices.

2. Integrating new microservices with the monolith via anti-corruption layers.

3. Strangling the monolith by identifying bounded contexts and extracting services.

Distributed systems

We compose distributed systems by:

1. Versioning, distributing, and refreshing configuration via a configuration server and management bus.

2. Dynamically discovering remote dependencies.

3. Decentralizing load balancing decisions.

4. Preventing cascading failures through circuit breakers and bulkheads.

5. Integrating on the behalf of specific clients via API Gateways.

Many additional helpful patterns exist, including those for automated testing and the construction of continuous delivery pipelines. For more information, the reader is invited to read "Testing Strategies in a Microservice Architecture" (*http://bit.ly/fowler-microtest*) by Toby Clemson and *Continuous Delivery: Reliable Software Releases through Build, Test, and Deployment Automation* by Jez Humble and David Farley (Addison-Wesley).

About the Author

Matt Stine is a technical product manager at Pivotal. He is a 15-year veteran of the enterprise IT industry, with experience spanning numerous business domains.

Matt is obsessed with the idea that enterprise IT "doesn't have to suck," and spends much of his time thinking about lean/agile software development methodologies, DevOps, architectural principles/patterns/practices, and programming paradigms, in an attempt to find the perfect storm of techniques that will allow corporate IT departments to not only function like startup companies, but also create software that delights users while maintaining a high degree of conceptual integrity. His current focus is driving Pivotal's solutions around supporting microservices architectures with Cloud Foundry and Spring.

Matt has spoken at conferences ranging from JavaOne to OSCON to YOW!, is a five-year member of the No Fluff Just Stuff tour, and serves as Technical Editor of *NFJS the Magazine*. Matt is also the founder and past president of the Memphis Java User Group.

CPSIA information can be obtained at www.ICGtesting.com
Printed in the USA
BVOW11s2211080415

395386BV00002B/3/P